CW00430179

ARNOLD NEWMAN

Pablo Picasso, Vallauris, France, 1954

THE GREAT PHOTOGRAPHERS

# ARNOLD NEWMAN

Robert A. Sobieszek

COLLINS

# ARNOLD NEWMAN

*by Robert A. Sobieszek*

Arnold Newman, self-portrait, 1979

The photographic portraiture of Arnold Newman has a very distinctive style. It is at once a style that is the result of many years of artistic training and practice, and a style which reflects a finely tuned, intuitive sensibility to people. It is a style that Newman, himself, once put into words quite cogently:

'A preoccupation with abstraction, combined with an interest in the documentation of people in their natural surroundings, was the basis upon which I built my approach to portraiture. The portrait of a personality must be as complete as we can make it. The physical image of the subject and the personality traits that image reflects are the most important aspects, but alone they are not enough. . . . We must also show the subject's relationship to his world either by fact or by graphic symbolism. The photographer's visual approach must weld these ideas into an organic whole, and the photographic image produced must create an atmosphere which reflects our impressions of the whole.' (From the introduction to his book *One Mind's Eye.*)

Like the best portraits regardless of medium, Newman's portraits record likeness, they reveal personality, and they symbolize character. His likenesses are both *faithful* and *interpretive.*

Newman's portrait of Stravinsky, his best known image (page 15), as well as those of Max Ernst (page 10), Piet Mondrian (page 17), Pablo Picasso (page 2), Alfred Stieglitz and Georgia O'Keeffe (page 11), Alfred Krupp (page 35), and Giorgio de Chirico (page 29) are not only some of the most accomplished photographic portraits, but they are even possibly more recognizable than the personality him or herself. Many of his portraits have become the symbolic distillation of the subject's appearance for the general public's consciousness. Certain of these pictures are the single likeness immediately equated with the personality and exemplify a very real artistic achievement in photographic portraiture, an achievement accomplished over the past four decades.

What differentiates this accomplishment from others in the same period is the precision of Newman's interpretive skills. For it is not simply the recognizable countenance that has made many of his photographs into essentially 'iconic' portraits. It is, of course, just as much the telling gesture or posture captured in the image; but it is also equally the perfect appropriateness of incidental accessories and physical setting that extend and enrich the portrait. In the finest photographs, the smallest details often assist the so-called principal subject in creating the image's force and beauty; even backgrounds can become foregrounds in the sense that without them, the foreground loses much of its significance. With Newman, the portrait is not just the human subject recorded, but the entire complex of interrelationships between the subject and its surroundings, its background, and its accessories. Indeed, in some of Newman's most striking portraits, such as those of I. M. Pei (page 32), Dr. Kurt Gödel (page 26), Louis Kahn (page 36), Grandma Moses (page 31) and Madame Sergei Koussevitzky (page 49), the human subject is so engulfed in meaningful details or salient environment that it occupies only the barest fraction of the image. Yet even in these extreme examples, Newman's fundamental genius holds everything together, yielding an extended portrait in which the character—personality as well as likeness—of the subject is intensely revealed.

Arnold Newman's portraits have already been included in many of the contemporary histories of photography and are quite comfortably placed within the context of the photographic portrait tradition. Since the advent of photography in the 1830s, rendering the human face has been the single most dominant role of the medium. The demand for likenesses that were both easy and inexpensive to obtain was clearly satisfied by the photograph from its earliest days. And the credibility of the camera image in no mean way contributed immensely to its popularity. In fact, it can be easily demonstrated that more portraits have been made by the camera than any other sort of picture.

The primary function of the camera portrait, throughout photography's history, has been to document the faces and figures of kin, acquaintances, and the famous. As such a record, the portrait becomes a visual biography, eliciting both immediate recognition when contemporary, and historical recollection when removed in time. The capacity of the photographic portrait to furnish us with amassed visual biographies was not only accepted but foreseen by the earliest photographers. William Henry Fox Talbot, the inventor of the modern process of negative/positive printing, inquired in his book *The Pencil of Nature* (1844–46): 'What could not be the value to our English Nobility of such a record of their ancestors who lived a century ago?' The tens and hundreds of thousands of photographic portraits that fill albums, scrapbooks and cupboard drawers testify to Talbot's prescience and to photography's phenomenal success as a vehicle for recording likeness. Countless photographs of barely identifiable individuals have been created, to be sure, with little art or expression and completely lacking in charm or picturesqueness. The role of these blandly ubiquitous images was and is clear: to simply record a face for another to consider and reflect upon.

In order to transcend the ubiquitous and the uninteresting, a relatively small percentage of portraitists have applied either the lessons of art or their own artistic sensibilities in creating something more than a mere record. These photographers have defined for us, over time, the limitations, possibilities, and attainments of the camera portrait as a work of art. Some have been purely amateur in their motivations while others have been visual artists struggling with their own mandated creativity. Their names constitute a pantheon of sorts: Degas, Lewis Carroll, Hugo Erfurth, David Octavius Hill and Robert Adamson, Julia Margaret Cameron, Edward Weston, Alfred Stieglitz, August Sander, and Diane Arbus, to list just a few. Still others have been strictly professional, balancing their own criteria of aesthetic judgements with the needs and demands of a client and a business. Yet they too share in the same pantheon: A. S. Southworth and J. J. Hawes, Nadar, Carjat, Franz Hanfstaengl, Cecil Beaton, Karsh of Ottawa, Edward Steichen, and Richard Avedon are just some of the more notable names, and in no way has their achievement been any less than the independent artist-photographer. A great portrait, whether palpable and material or metaphoric and abstract, is still a record of a human; it matters little if done for private needs or for those of a client.

*A great portrait is still a record of a human.*

Essentially a professional photographer, Arnold Newman has maintained the biographical imperative of the portrait photograph: 'The portrait is a form of biography. Its purpose is to inform now and to record for history. We must record facts, not fiction or idealized images. The vital visual facts in today's magazine make up tomorrow's history textbook.'

Like Talbot before him, Newman firmly believes that the fundamental purpose of the portrait is to record a given likeness, and he has even given the British a record of their future ancestors, as it were, when he published his *The Great British* in 1979. Newman, however, goes well beyond Talbot's apparently simplistic faith in the mere likeness and its recognizability. Newman does not accept that any likeness will suffice nor that the content is most important. Before any portrait can be a good portrait, he has claimed repeatedly, it has to be a good photograph, which is why the very best portraits are achieved by the most sensitive photographers.

'The physical image of the subject,' Newman has stated, 'and the personality traits that image reflects are the most important aspects, *but alone they are not enough.'* [Emphasis added.] As an impetus to immediate recognition or as a matrix for historical recollection, any portrait may be effective. As a vital work of art and as an image that expresses as much as it records, the photographic portrait requires being much more. This does not, certainly, mean that the good portrait needs to be filled with extraneous matter, but rather that its organic whole communicate more than just the superficial resemblance of the sitter. The most artistically successful portrait photographs can range from a simple countenance to a complex arrangement of material and symbolic information. The portrait can be neutral and clinical, wherein the figure or face of the subject is the only discernible content; there are no props or furnishings and the background is a void, a blank foil advancing the figure into an abstract space to subsist there by itself. Many of the most prosaic daguerreotypes are absolutely compelling just because of their lack of environment and props, and some of the daguerreian masterpieces by Southworth and Hawes and by Sabatier-Blot are redoubly expressive because these artists capitalized on this aesthetic effect. Certain of Julia Margaret Cameron's greatest portraits also exhibit what might be called this primacy of physiognomy, as do those by Nadar and, more recently, Richard Avedon and Robert Mapplethorpe.

Man on the porch of a church, West Palm Beach, Florida, 1941

The good photographic portrait, alternatively, can be attained by the appropriate and sensitive cohesion of symbolically expressive information. Gestures, facial expressions, physical accessories, emotive lighting and environmental contexts can each carry with it a symbolic charge that conveys a sense about the subject beyond the strictly physical look of the face. Symbolically, the likeness is accorded a fuller set of associations and subtexts about the character and meaning of the subject than were that subject to be photographed as an isolated incident of humanity. Historically, the most common symbolic gesture has been the inclusion of some token object or set of accessories that in some fashion say something about the subject's occupation or status in the community. The book on the table in nineteenth century daguerreotypes, the antique statue or column behind the sitter in *fin-de-siècle* portraits, the tools in the sitter's hands as in the portraits of social types by August Sander, and the superbly elegant fashions worn by socially prominent subjects since the beginnings of photography, are all expressive parentheses about the assumed or real character of the sitter. Each of these artifacts signals a quality of the sitter and inspires the viewer to an understanding of the subject's social situation, degree of intelligence, and other implied biographical details.

The advantage of the accessory or the fashions to be worn by the sitter is that they can be brought into the photographer's studio for the sitting, or even stocked by the artist in his studio for the patron. More difficult is the symbolic use of the physical context or environment to convey some message about the portrait's subject. Painted backdrops can be used of course, but these are for the most part obviously fictitious and patently false. Only with the amateur snapshot does the natural environment of the subject most commonly present itself with the sitter at the time of photographing; at home or on vacation, the background information is revealing of the subject's place at that moment. The professional photographer, on the other hand, has to search out and locate the sitter within the most telling, appropriate, and most discursive situation. For the environment in which the sitter exists within the image, the enclosing architecture or cohabited landscape, informs the viewer with an understanding of the sitter and an appreciation of the sitter's circumstances. Andy Warhol is, in a photograph by Avedon, a personality who just happens to be an artist; Max Ernst, in a portrait by Newman (page 10), is a surrealist artist at home, made manifest by his collection of paintings and Kachina dolls and subtended by the Loplop shape of his cigarette smoke. Both portraits are expressive, but textually one is fuller and more informational than the other; one is a sonnet, the other a novella.

It is precisely the working out of the relationships that exist between a person and his environment that is the basis for Newman's portraiture. Around 1941, when Newman began to make portraits, there were few photographers attempting to integrate the sitter with his or her natural surroundings. It was with this notion of integration in mind, an idea Newman often ascribes as basic to the fundamental structure of the amateur snapshot, that he commenced his career as portraitist, first with artists and later broadening his choices to include other subjects. He was not by any means the first to entertain this objective. As early as 1884, J. P. Mayall published his portfolio of portraits entitled *Artists at Home*; Erich Salomon made history with his journalistic portrayals of politicians gathering together in conference rooms; August Sander's work is replete with portraits of people at work or at home; and Brassaï had begun his long involvement with picturing artists in their studios as early as 1932. But, to be fair, in the early 1940s, Mayall's work was practically unknown, Salomon's was seen as primarily examples of a successful application of the then new 35mm camera, and Brassaï's portraits of Picasso, Matisse, and Dali were not widely circulated. For the most part, the professional portrait was a studio matter in which the sitter was dramatically severed from his or her natural *milieu,* or it was taken out of doors where the setting accomplished little by way of extending the definition of the subject. One has only to think of the Hollywood portraits of the 1930s, such as those by George Hoyningen-Huené and Hurrell, or the avant-garde portraits by Helmar Lerski, Umbo, and Man Ray.

*Newman was a pioneer of environmental or extended portraiture.*

Essentially, therefore, Arnold Newman can be considered as a pioneer in the practice of environmental or extended portraiture. At their best, these integrative portraits function for Newman on a somewhat symbolic level, and he is quite convinced that the isolation of these people in their surroundings is almost in itself a symbol. The symbolism is not a factor that is constructed out of the particular details and data of the portrait. Rather, the complex relationships of figure and environment act as a pictorial code to the personality of the subject and as a demarcation of his or her character. Thus, such elusive material information as the glowing industrial depths behind the figure of Alfred Krupp (page 35), the searing luminescence of the lamp hanging over Jean Cocteau's head (page 43), the scummy, discoloured wall behind the profile of Jean Dubuffet (page 19), the optical fall-off arching across the sky above Edward Hopper (page 21), the solemn darkness in the Georges Rouault portraits (page 27), the notational and almost musical light patterns behind Madame Koussevitzky (page 49), and the absolute emptiness of the wall and dancer's barre behind the figure of Martha Graham (page 47) are not merely suggestive bits of decoration but essential to the symbolic delineation of the subject's being. All the factors within the portrait, whether concrete or subjective, legible or felt, signs or moods, contribute to the pictorial penetration of who and what the subject may be.

A great deal of the psychological trust in photographic portraiture has been combined with the cultural assumption that the human face is a vehicle for the individual's character. In 1850, the German philosopher Schopenhauer could write: 'That the outer man is a picture of the inner, and the face an expression and revelation of the whole character, is a presumption likely enough in itself, and therefore a safe one to go by; borne out as it is by the fact that people are always anxious to see anyone who has made himself famous . . . photography . . . affords the most complete satisfaction of our curiosity.'

Taken to an extreme during the last century, the camera's image was periodically thought to be able to actually elicit and capture the sitter's inner personality. Nathaniel Hawthorne's daguerreotypist, Holgrave, in *The House of Seven Gables* (1851), talked at length about the penetrating insight of the daguerreotype portrait and claimed simply that 'while we give it credit only for depicting the merest surface, it actually brings out the secret character with a truth that no painter would ever venture upon, even could he detect it'. Even in this century, Arnold Newman recalls a conversation he had with his friend, the painter Ben Shahn, about the daguerreotype portrait. According to Newman, Shahn 'thought that during the long exposures required for the daguerreotype, the sitter would have many and different thoughts and these gradually settled the expression "most typically" of the sitter'.

Yaacov Agam, collage, New York City, 1966–72

The majority of accomplished portraitists have admitted that a necessary requirement for a good portrait was to be found in the photographer's ability to interpret the sitter and render not only a likeness but one which contained a clue to the sitter's inner character. Writing in the same year that Hawthorne's novel was published, the French critic Francis Wey attempted the very first art theory of the photographic portrait and, in it, stressed that 'resemblance is not a mechanical reproduction but an interpretation that translates for the eyes the image of an object so that the spirit imagines it with the aid of memory'. For him, the interpretive skills of the photographer made the image more a likeness of the subject than the subject himself. 'Let us not be afraid,' he declared, 'to affirm that, materially speaking, the copy of a figure is susceptible of seizing a spectator by the power of the interpretation more vividly than even the reality could under certain circumstances.'

The idea of the interpretive portrait—that portrait which captures something of the inner personality of the sitter, that image which attempts to reveal a bit of the subject's interior being or soul—has been central to the photographic portrait tradition. The French photographer Nadar stated it most simply when he said that 'the portrait I do best is that of the man I know the best'. In 1910, the American critic A. J. Anderson wrote: 'The gift of character reading is essential in the portrait photographer; and once the sitter's character is discovered, it is no bad plan to try and photograph some predominant quality in the abstract.' Most good portraiture goes well beyond the superficial recording of the subject's features; it interprets and by so doing transcends what Julia Margaret Cameron denounced as 'mere conventional topographic photography—map making and skeleton rendering of feature and form'. At the same time, most photographers have also admitted that any single portrait interpretation is but a single, individual and, for the most part, incomplete analysis or interpretation.

*Nadar, the French photographer, said 'the portrait I do best is that of the man I know the best'.*

Arnold Newman is 'convinced that any photographic attempt to show the complete man is nonsense, to an extent. We can only show, as best we can, what

*continued on page 58*

# THE PHOTOGRAPHS

Max Ernst, New York City, 1942

Georgia O'Keeffe and Alfred Stieglitz, New York City, 1944

Yasuo Kuniyoshi, New York City, 1941

Moses and Raphael Soyer, New York City, 1942

Jean Arp, New York City, 1949

Igor Stravinsky, New York City, 1946

J. Robert Oppenheimer, Berkeley, California, 1948

Piet Mondrian, New York City, 1942

Marc Chagall, New York City, 1941

Jean Dubuffet, Vence, France, 1956

Milton Avery, New York City, 1961

Edward Hopper, Truro, Massachusetts, 1960

Alexander Calder, Roxbury, Connecticut, 1957

Haile Selassie I, Emperor of Ethiopia, Addis Ababa, 1958

President John F. Kennedy, Washington, D.C., 1961

David Ben-Gurion, Tel Aviv, 1967

Kurt Gödel, Institute for Advanced Study, Princeton, New Jersey, 1956

Georges Rouault, Paris, 1957

David Hare, Provincetown, Massachusetts, 1952

Giorgio de Chirico, Rome, 1957

Leonard Bernstein, Avery Fisher Hall, New York City, 1968

Grandma Moses, Eagle Bridge, New York, 1949

I. M. Pei, New York City, 1967

Aaron Copland, Peekskill, New York, 1959

Willem de Kooning, Springs, New York, 1978

Alfred Krupp, Essen, West Germany, 1963

Louis Kahn in front of Yale University Art Gallery, New Haven, Connecticut, 1964

Frank Stella, New York City, 1967

David Hockney, London, 1978

Joan Miró, Palma, Majorca, Spain, 1979

Cardinal Enrique Pla Y Daniel, Primate of the Spanish Church, Toledo, Spain, 1964

Georgia O'Keeffe, Ghost Ranch, New Mexico, 1968

Sir Frederick Ashton, London, 1978

Jean Cocteau, Paris, 1960

Paul Strand, New York City, 1966

Ansel Adams, Carmel, California, 1976

Adolph Gottlieb, New York City, 1970

Martha Graham, New York City, 1961

Henry Geldzahler, New York City, 1972

Madame Sergei Koussevitzky, New York City, 1960

Carl Sandburg, New York City, 1959

Marilyn Monroe, Beverly Hills, California, 1962

Sir John Gielgud and Sir Ralph Richardson, London, 1978

Sir Cecil Beaton, Broad Chalke, Salisbury, 1978

Bill Brandt, London, 1978

Henry Moore, collage, Much Hadham, Hertfordshire, 1966–72

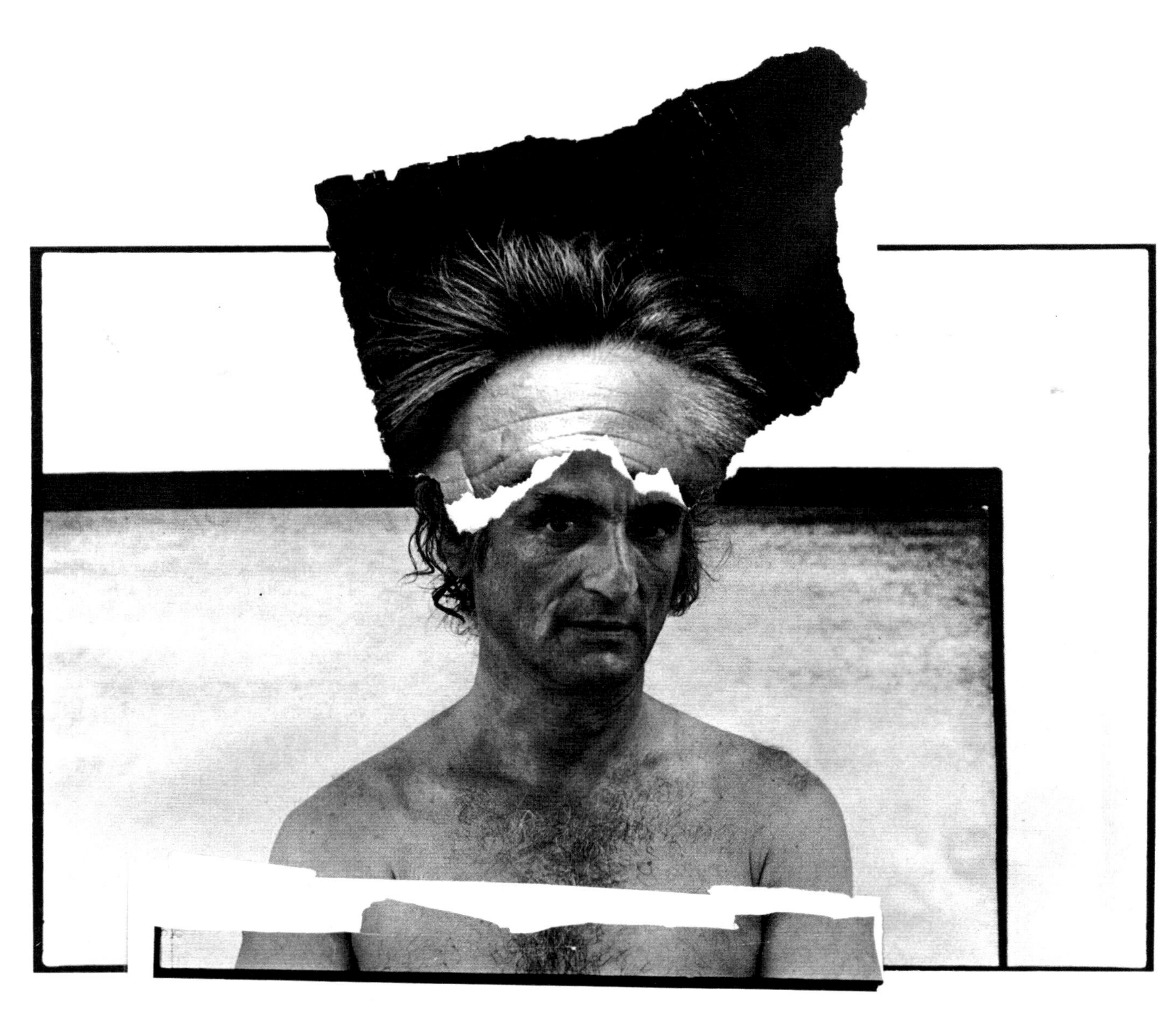

Larry Rivers, collage, South Hampton, New York, 1975

Andy Warhol, collage, New York City, 1973–74

*continued from page 8*
the outer man reveals; the inner man is seldom revealed to anyone, sometimes not even to the man himself. We have to interpret, but our interpretation can be false, of course. We can impose our own feelings upon a man, and these feelings can do him a great injustice—we cannot always be one hundred percent correct. I think one of the greatest tests of the portrait photographer is his intuitiveness, his ability to judge a person, his ability to get along with all kinds of people, from a street-car conductor to a prime minister of a world power, his ability to have sympathy for each man and to understand the man he is photographing, to show tact and understanding of the problem the man obviously faces being before the camera. . . . photography is a matter of creative *selection*. A portrait photographer, or any photographer for that matter, must be selective because he [is] limited [by the] material in front of him. . . . Inevitably there is a great deal of the photographer in his finished product. . . . If there isn't much of him, then there isn't much of a portrait. In other words, the photographer must be a part of the picture. It's a matter of joining forces with the sitter, in a sense.'

*'The photographer must be a part of the picture. It's a matter of joining forces with the sitter, in a sense.'*

For Newman, then, interpretation must be, in order to be effective, a combination of knowledge or judgement on the one hand and intuition on the other, and the most useful intuitiveness is largely based on a well-integrated pre-knowledge, tact, and understanding. Nadar had to know the sitter fairly well in order to do a good portrait. One of the greatest American daguerreotypists, A. S. Southworth has provided us with what is perhaps the best definition of the manner in which the portrait photographer intuits his subject: 'What is to be done is obliged to be done quickly. The whole character of the sitter is to be read at first sight; the whole likeness, as it shall appear when finished, is to be seen at first, in each and all its details, and in their unity and combinations . . . in the result there is to be no departure from truth in the delineation and representation of beauty and expression, and character.'

The important point here is not just the quickness with which the photographer works his magic, but also just how well he can 'read' the sitter's character, or as Newman would say, 'his ability to judge a person . . . to have sympathy for each man and to understand the man he is photographing'.

Newman readily admits to the important role that intuition plays in his photography. 'Strictly speaking, we should know as much as possible about the person from many sources; if he's well known, we may get the information from the printed page; if he's not well known, we may find it by visiting him and talking to friends and associates and going out to lunch or dinner beforehand, and so forth. This naturally helps, but sometimes . . . the man walks in on you cold, or you must walk in on the man and his environment cold. In that case, you have only your intuition and the background of experience you have amassed over the years to help you make the judgements.'

The personality of the sitter is never static, and it is even questionable whether anyone maintains a single, definite character throughout their lives. Realizing this, previous centuries distinguished between the static 'physiognomy' (the likeness at any given moment) and the mobile, and much more difficult to read 'pathognomy' (the likeness through time). Consequently, no single portrait could ever really capture the inner essence of the subject nor is there any such thing as a complete portrait of an individual. Each portrait is nothing more than a rendering of a person's likeness at a particular point in time. Inspired and revealing it may be, but it reveals only a constantly changing character at a precise location and at a specific moment and, not less importantly, that character posed in front of a camera and viewed by another person. Newman is fully conscious of this aspect of portrait photography.

'It seems to me that no one picture can ever be a final summation of a personality. There are so many facets in every human being that it is impossible to present them all in one photograph. When I make a portrait, I don't *take* a photograph. I *build* it, seeking all those graphic elements that will express the most typical common denominator of the subject as I see him within the obvious limitations of a single image.' What is important, therefore, to the formulation of a portrait is the precise distillation of what exactly connotes and denotes the person portrayed. Newman labels this the 'common denominator of the subject', and few have phrased it more aptly.

Any successful portrait photograph is the result of the symbiotic relationship that comes to exist between the photographer and the subject. The sitter's ability to actively affect the photographer's approach to his portrait has been a commonly understood psychological relationship. The plebeian portraitist will usually allow the subject complete power over the picture, from conception to the final print. The more artistically exceptional photographer will use this relationship as a creative matrix in which to motivate his own concerns and treatment of the portrait. The more conscientious the photographer is, the more the finished print will be the product of a controlled yet receptive vision.

Newman's utter control is not commanding but, rather, sympathetic. He allows his subjects to place themselves and to relax into their most characteristic postures with a minimum of staging, overt direction, or choreography. In order to diminish the customary self-consciousness of the subject, he will often spend preliminary sessions conversing with the subject and observing his or her gestures, facial expressions, and postures. With these observations in mind, and with some measure of understanding the character of the subject, Newman then selects the most appropriate setting and its details, and gently guides the subject to assume the most potentially revealing relationships with that environment. The observing photographer is, however, not merely the pawn of the observed sitter. Newman leaves little to chance, and only infrequently accepts a post-visualized accident. Whether the portrait is minimal and geometric, sensuous and enigmatic, or baroque and dense, he maintains a complete visual domination of every formal aspect of the final print; the set-up, the lighting, the cropping of the image, and the printing values are not choices made by the sitter. The sitters share in the revealing of themselves to the photographer; the photographer is responsible for the work of art.

*'When I make a portrait, I don't* take *a photograph . . . I* build *it.'*

Observing the nuances of behaviour, posing the sitter by indirection, staging the shot by selection, and, finally, intuiting the most revealing moment to photograph —these, then, are what constitute the art of Arnold Newman, and the manner in which he has interpreted some of the greats of our time. Newman's work is clearly within the tradition of photographic portraiture as it has developed for more than a century. In a number of ways there are parallels and similarities between his 'common denominator of the subject' and the sense of personality inherent in some early daguerreotypes, the portraits by Carjat and Nadar, and those by Victor Regnault or Hill and Adamson. But whereas the nineteenth century photographer, when he thought about the art of photography, frequently based his aesthetics largely on the arts of painting or print-making, Newman is entirely in line with twentieth century photographic art theory.

## Technical note

Arnold Newman makes a very crisp appraisal of the part played by equipment and materials in his photography. To him, they are simply the tools through which he expresses the ideas and instincts that are the core of his work.

Over the years he has used a wide variety of cameras, from large-format view models to 35mm SLR's, drawing on a full range of different focal-length lenses. He likes to use natural lighting whenever possible but often has to augment or balance it with artificial illumination, either tungsten or flash.

He selects whatever photographic tools are necessary for the job in hand and its specific problems. 'There are no rules for techniques,' he once said, 'only solutions'. When necessary he will crop the picture format to strengthen an image and he is bold enough to use even more radical methods of controlling the finished photograph, for instance, through collage or even by partially tearing a print.

'Always remember,' he says, 'you do not make photographs with cameras and film, you make them with your brain and your heart and your stomach'.

'We must see our subjects through the camera,' says Newman, 'and not through the eyes of one who thinks in terms of another medium. . . . The subject of a photographic portrait must be envisioned in terms of sharp lenses, fast emulsions, textures, light and realism. He must be thought of in terms of the twentieth century, of houses he lives in and places he works, in terms of the kind of light the windows in these places let through and by which we see him every day. We must think of him in the way he sits and the way he stands in everyday life, not just when he is before the camera. This is thinking in terms of photography. We are perhaps not consciously producing an art form, but in clear thinking, at least we are creating, not imitating.'

Throughout his career as a photographer, Newman has consistently adhered to this notion. He has adhered to it, but he has not just given us a number of artistically glamorous photographic portraits. He has also, and this must be stressed, compiled a veritable compendium of significant *iconographies* that at once both counters and compliments his achievement as an artist. His portraits are excellent portraits whatever one's criteria of aesthetic judgement; they are at the same time an encyclopaedic index to the likenesses of many important personalities. Both factors have been at mutual play in the realization of his art, and both will continue to be seriously entertained as comments on the history of the era. That Arnold Newman has recorded these faces is because he is a photographer; that his pictures are constructed so eloquently and signify so much aesthetically is because he is an artist.

# Chronology

**1918**
Born on 3 March in New York City.

**1920–34**
Lived in Atlantic City, New Jersey. Began his art studies.

**1936–38**
Studied art at the University of Miami, Coral Gables, Florida.

**1938**
Worked as assistant in portrait studio, Philadelphia, Pennsylvania.

**1939**
Met Alfred Stieglitz. Began work as a photographic studio manager at Tooley-Myron Photo Studio in West Palm Beach, Florida.

**1941–42**
Received encouragements from Beaumont Newhall and Alfred Stieglitz. Moved to New York City. Museum of Modern Art purchased prints. Began 'experimental' portraits using artists as models.

**1942–45**
Operated his own studio in Miami Beach. Continued photographing artists in New York.

**1945–46**
One-man exhibition, 'Artists Look Like This', at Philadelphia Museum of Art.

**1946**
Moved to New York and set up Arnold Newman Studios, Inc, New York. Worked for *Harper's Bazaar, Fortune,* and *Life*. Took his famous photograph of Stravinsky.

**1949**
Married Augusta Rubenstein. Took photographs for *Portfolio*.

**1951**
One-man exhibition, Camera Club, New York. Began series of advertisements for *New York Times* (to continue until 1958). Began work for *Holiday*. Received Photokina Award in Cologne.

**1954**
Visited Paris. Photographed Picasso in Vallauris.

**1955**
One-man exhibition, Limelight Gallery, New York.

**1958**
Travelled to Africa to photograph tribal and modern leaders.

**1963**
Photographed Stravinsky again. Awarded gold medal for exhibition at Biennale Internazionale della Fotografia, Venice.

**1965**
Appointed as adviser on photography by Israel Museum, Jerusalem.

**1967**
Published *Bravo Stravinsky*.

**1974**
Published *One Mind's Eye*.

**1975**
Given Life Achievement Award by American Society of Magazine Photographers.

**1978**
Commissioned by National Portrait Gallery, London to photograph 'The Great British'.

**1979**
'The Great British' exhibited in London and at Light Gallery, New York, and book published.

**1980**
Published *Artists: Portraits from Four Decades*.

**1981**
Received honorary degree from University of Miami. Made extensive tour of Australia and Japan.

**1984**
Working on a large exhibition to include his abstractions as well as portraits.

# Bibliography

## By Arnold Newman

### Books


*Happytown Tales*, with Laurence Tremblay; Parker Art Printing Association, Coral Gables, Florida, 1944 (drawings by Arnold Newman).

*Bravo Stravinsky*, with text by Robert Craft; World, Cleveland, Ohio, 1967.

*One Mind's Eye: The Portraits and Other Photographs of Arnold Newman*, foreword by Beaumont Newhall, introduction by Robert Sobieszek; New York Graphic Society, Boston, and Secker & Warburg, London, 1974 (includes extensive bibliography).

*Faces U.S.A.*, introduction by Thomas Thompson; Amphoto, New York, 1976.

*The Great British*, foreword by John Hayes, introduction by George Perry; New York Graphic Society, Boston, and Weidenfeld & Nicholson, London, 1979.

*Artists: Portraits from Four Decades*, foreword by Henry Geldzahler, introduction by Arnold Newman; New York Graphic Society, 1980, Boston, and Weidenfeld & Nicholson, London, 1981.


### Selected Magazine Articles


'Portrait of an Artist', *Minicam Photography*, Cincinnati, Ohio, November 1945.

'Portrait Assignment', *Photo Arts*, Spring 1948.

'Speaking of Portraits . . .', *Universal Photo Almanac*, 1952.

'Arnold Newman's Europe', *Popular Photography*, New York, March 1964.

'Peer Group', *Camera Arts*, New York, January/February 1981.


## About Arnold Newman

### Books


*The History of Photography from 1839 to the Present Day*, Beaumont Newhall, New York, 1949.

*Famous Portraits*, L. Fritz Gruber, New York, 1960 (published as *Fame*, London, 1960).

*The Encyclopedia of Photography*, H. M. Kinzer, New York, 1964.

*The Picture History of Photography*, Peter Pollack, New York, 1969.

*Looking at Photographs: 100 pictures from the Collection of the Museum of Modern Art*, John Szarkowski, New York, 1973.

*The Magic Image: The Genius of Photography from 1839 to the Present Day*, Cecil Beaton & Gail Buckland, London, 1975.

*Faces: A Narrative History of the Portrait in Photography*, Ben Maddow, Boston, 1977.

*The Best of Popular Photography*, New York, 1979.

*Current Biography*, vol. 41, Charles Moritz, New York, 1980.

*World Photography: 25 Contemporary Masters Write About Their Work, Techniques and Equipment*, Bryn Campbell, London and New York, 1981.

*Master Photographers*, Pat Booth, London and New York, 1983.


### Selected Magazine Articles


'Arnold Newman', Fritz Neugass, *Camera*, June 1953.

'On Assignment with Arnold Newman', Arthur Goldsmith, *Popular Photography*, May 1957.

'American Artists Photographed by Arnold Newman', Nan Rosenthal, *Art in America*, June 1965.

'Les têtes couronnées d'Arnold Newman', Evelyne Jesenof, *Photo* (French edition), June 1973.

'Arnold Newman: The Portrait as Record and Interpretation', Arthur Goldsmith, *Popular Photography*, November 1973.

'Arnold Newman', Trevor Gett, *Australian Photography*, October 1980.

'Arnold Newman', Par Rittsel, *Foto Start Bildnummer*, July/August 1982.


### Film


*The Image Makers: The Environment of Arnold Newman*, Nebraska Educational Television Network, 1977.


## Exhibitions

### Individual Shows

**1941** A.D. Gallery, New York (with Ben Rose).
**1945** 'Artists Look Like This', Philadelphia Museum of Art (later toured throughout USA).
**1951** Camera Club, New York.
**1955** Limelight Gallery, New York.
**1963** 'Portraits', Biennale Internazionale della Fotografia, Venice.
**1972** Light Gallery, New York.
'Photographs from Three Decades', International Museum of Photography, George Eastman House, Rochester, New York (later toured throughout USA; in 1980 to Japan).
**1974** 'One Mind's Eye', Light Gallery, New York.
**1975** David Mirvish Gallery, Toronto, Canada.
**1976** Galerie Fiolet, Amsterdam.
**1977** 'Arnold Newman—Recent Photographs', Light Gallery, New York.
**1978** 'Portraits', Israel Museum, Jerusalem.
'Portraits', Tel Aviv Museum of Art.
Moderna Museet, Stockholm.
**1979** 'The Great British', National Portrait Gallery, London.
'The Great British', Light Gallery, New York.
Venezia '79, La Fotografia, Venice.
**1980** 'Artists: Portraits from Four Decades', Light Gallery, New York.
Lowe Art Museum, University of Miami, Coral Gables, Florida.
**1981** Photo Gallery International, Tokyo.
**1982** Yuen Lui Gallery, Seattle, Washington.
Hills Gallery, Denver, Colorado.
Clarence Street Lighthouse, Melbourne, Australia.
**1984** Daniel Wolf Gallery, New York.

### Group Shows

**1943** 'Masters of Photography', Museum of Modern Art, New York.
**1948** 'In and Out of Focus', Museum of Modern Art, N.Y.
**1953** 'Contemporary American Photography', National Museum of Modern Art, Tokyo.
**1957** 'Faces in American Art', Metropolitan Museum of Art, N.Y.
**1959** 'Photography at Mid-Century', International Museum of Photography, George Eastman House, Rochester, N.Y.
**1964** 'The Photographer's Eye', Museum of Modern Art, N.Y.
**1968** 'Photography in the 20th Century', National Gallery of Canada, Ottawa (toured in Canada and USA to 1973).
**1970** 'The Camera and the Human Facade', Smithsonian Institution, Washington DC.
**1972** 'Portrait of the Artists', Metropolitan Museum of Art, N.Y.

### Public Collections

Metropolitan Museum of Art, New York.
International Museum of Photography, George Eastman House, Rochester, New York.
Philadelphia Museum of Art.
Smithsonian Institution, Washington DC.
Art Institute of Chicago.
National Portrait Gallery, London.
Moderna Museet, Stockholm.
Israel Museum, Jerusalem.

*Index of photographs*

## Author

**Robert A. Sobieszek** is Director of Photographic Collections at the International Museum of Photography at George Eastman House, Rochester, New York. An art historian, he received his graduate degrees from Stanford University, California and Columbia University, New York. He has written articles which have appeared internationally on 19th and 20th century photography as well as on fibre arts and metalwork. He is the author of a number of books including *The Spirit of Fact* (1976), *British Masters of the Albumen Print* (1976), *Photography and Other Questions* (1983) and *The Architectural Photography of Hedrich-Blessing* (1984).

## Series Consultant Editors

**Romeo Martinez** has worked in photographic journalism for over 50 years. Resident in Paris, he is the author of several books on the history of photography and is the editor of the *Bibliothek der Photographie* series. He was responsible for the relaunch on the international market of the magazine *Camera*. From 1957 to 1965, he organized the biennial photographic exhibitions in Venice. Romeo Martinez organized the iconographic department at the Pompidou Centre in Paris. He is a member of the Administration Council and of the Art Commission of the Societé Français de Photographie and a member of the Deutsche Gesellschaft für Photographie.

**Bryn Campbell** has been active both as a professional photographer and as an editor and writer on photography. He is known to many as the presenter of the BBC TV series *Exploring Photography*. As a photographer, he has worked for a Fleet Street agency, with *The Observer*, and on assignments for *Geo* and *The Observer Magazine*. He has been Assistant Editor of *Practical Photography* and of *Photo News Weekly*, Editor of *Cameras & Equipment*, Deputy Editor of *The British Journal of Photography* and, from 1964 to 1966, Picture Editor of *The Observer*.

In 1974 he was made an Honorary Associate Lecturer in Photographic Arts at the Polytechnic of Central London. The same year he was appointed a Trustee of the Photographers' Gallery, London. He served on the Photography Sub-Committee of the Arts Council and later became a member of the Art Panel. He is a Fellow of the Institute of Incorporated Photographers and a Fellow of the Royal Photographic Society. His book *World Photography* was published in 1981.

First published in 1984 by
William Collins Sons & Co Ltd

London · Glasgow · Sydney
Auckland · Johannesburg



ISBN 0 00 411955 X

Typesetting by Chambers Wallace, London
Printed in Italy